The
BATHROOM FUNNY STUFF BOOK

————— • —————

by

Russ Edwards & Jack Kreismer

RED-LETTER PRESS, INC.
Saddle River, New Jersey

THE BATHROOM FUNNY STUFF BOOK
Print Date 2013
COPYRIGHT ©2012 Red-Letter Press, Inc.
ISBN-13: 978-1-60387-001-6
ISBN: 1-60387-001-6

Red-Letter Press, Inc.
P.O. Box 393
Saddle River, NJ 07458

www.Red-LetterPress.com

ACKNOWLEDGMENTS

EDITORIAL:
Jeff Kreismer

•

BOOK DESIGN & TYPOGRAPHY:
Jeff Kreismer

•

COVER & CONTENT ART:
Behum Graphics

•

CONTRIBUTORS:
Sherry Kazeleski
Jerry Miller
Kobus Reyneke
Mike Ryan
Lori Walsh

The traffic was backed up even more than usual and people were getting out of their cars to find out what was up. Dave strolled up to the motorist ahead of him and asked what was going on.

"Apparently, some nut hijacked a bus load of lawyers and is holding them for ransom. He says he wants $10,000 or he'll douse the bus with gasoline and set it on fire. These guys with the buckets are taking up a collection."

"Oh really?" Dave said with concern. "How much is everyone giving?"

The motorist replied, "About a gallon."

Patient: Doctor, I keep seeing double!

Doctor: Please, have a seat on the couch.

Patient: Which one?

Rarely is the questioned asked:
Is our children learning?
-George W. Bush

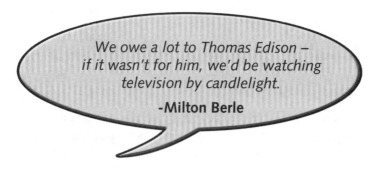

*We owe a lot to Thomas Edison –
if it wasn't for him, we'd be watching
television by candlelight.*

-Milton Berle

Patient: Doc, I broke my arm in two places!

Doctor: Don't go back to those places.

A fellow goes into a bakery known for fashioning custom-made cakes. He says, "I'd like to have a cake made in the shape of the letter S."

The baker says he can do it, but at a premium. The fellow tells the baker not to worry, price is no object. The baker advises the fellow that he'll need about four hours.

The customer returns at the appointed time and the baker unveils the S shaped cake, one in a beautiful block letter. The customer is upset, though. He says, "I want it to look fancier. Can't you make it in cursive script?"

The baker says, "Absolutely. Give me another three hours."

The fellow returns a few hours later and the baker shows him a beautifully designed cake in the shape of a scripted S, outlined in red and green frosting. The fellow is still upset. "It looks too much like Christmas. Can you make that frosting yellow?"

The baker says, "Sure. Come back in half an hour."

The fellow comes back once again, the baker shows him the cake, and it finally meets with his approval. As the baker starts to put it in the box, the fellow says, "Don't do that. I'm gonna eat it here."

The boss is in the middle of interviewing a managerial candidate and decides it's time for a character check. He says to the guy, "Let's assume that you go to my house and my wife invites you in, but tells you that I won't be home for another few hours. What would you do?"

The job applicant thinks for a moment and says, "Would you mind showing me a picture of her?"

I was so ugly my mother used to feed me with a slingshot.

-Rodney Dangerfield

The only way to keep your health is to eat what you don't want, drink what you don't like, and do what you'd rather not.

-Mark Twain

Johnny Jokes #1

Q: What do you call an igloo without a toilet?
A: An ig.

•••

Did you hear about Robin Hood's house?
It has a little John.

•••

A sweet, blue-haired old granny went to the doctor and reported that she hadn't had a bowel movement in two weeks. "I go and sit in the bathroom for an hour in the morning and an hour at night."

"Have you taken anything?" queried the MD.

"Yes I have," replied the granny. "A book."

•••

Q: How many men does it take to change a roll of toilet paper?
A: Nobody knows- it's never happened.

A guest from Montreal was staying at a little bed and breakfast near Toronto. He called down to the clerk and asked for some pepper.

"Will that be black pepper or white pepper sir?" asked his host.

A bit annoyed, the guest answered, "Toilette Pepper!"

•••

Contrary to popular belief, Thomas Edison did not invent the light bulb. Long before Edison's time, a Native American, tired of hearing people stumble around in the outhouse at night, discovered electricity and equipped an outhouse with electric lights. This made him the first person in history to wire a head for a reservation.

•••

Mike the plumber was working in the bathroom when the owner popped her head in and said, "Will it be alright if I have a bath while you're having your lunch?"

"Knock yourself out lady," replied Mike, "as long as you don't splash my sandwiches."

Always end the name of your child with a vowel, so that when you yell the name will carry.

-Bill Cosby

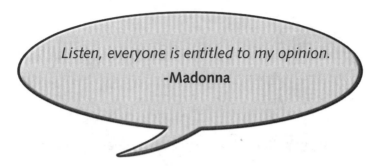

Listen, everyone is entitled to my opinion.
-Madonna

And then there was the schoolteacher who was arrested at the airport for attempting to go through security with a slide rule and a calculator. He was charged with carrying weapons of math instruction.

A woman, picking through the frozen turkeys at the supermarket, asked the stock boy, "Do these turkeys get any bigger?"

The stock boy answered, "No ma'am, they're dead."

"Mommy! Mommy!" little Johnny exclaimed as he ran in the door. "Today on the bus Daddy said I should give up my seat for a lady."

"Well, that is very nice and polite," smiled his mother.

"Yeah," said little Johnny, "but I was sitting on his lap."

Billionaire Ronald Rump was scheduled to be picked up by helicopter from atop a Manhattan skyscraper, taken to a private jet and then fly on to Europe. He parked his Roll Royce in front of the skyscraper, and went into the bank lobby to request a loan of $5,000.

The loan officer instantly recognized him but as per the bank's policy, had to ask for collateral and so "The Rump", as he liked to call himself, handed over the keys to his Rolls which was moved to the security of the underground parking garage for safekeeping.

A couple of weeks later Rump returned and paid the loan in full plus the $15 interest. Before handing over the keys, however, the loan officer simply had to ask a question.

"Mr. Rump, you have a Rolls Royce, a helicopter and private jet. I know that you are worth billions. Why then did you need to borrow $5,000?"

"Oh I didn't need the money," Rump answered, "but where else could I park a Rolls Royce in Manhattan for two weeks on $15?"

A recent police study found that you're much more likely to get shot by a fat cop if you run.

-Dennis Miller

Anyone who says he can see through women is missing a lot.

-Groucho Marx

A drop-dead gorgeous girl says to the owner of the dress shop, "May I try on that dress in the window?"

"Sure," he says, "it'll be great for business!"

On a Facebook Wall:
"Dear Son, How are you? We are all doing fine and we miss you. Now please turn off the computer and come down for dinner!"

Two geeks met for lunch at the local Internet cafe and one of them could hardly contain himself. "You won't believe what happened to me today," he said excitedly.

"You do seem stoked, Man," replied his friend.

"It was amazing- a girl rode up to me on her bike, took off all her clothes and said 'Take whatever you want.'"

"Awesome!" replied his buddy.

"Yeah, so I took her bike."

His friend nodded and said, "Good idea, Dude. The clothes probably wouldn't have fit you anyway."

A grandmother was watching her grandson play in the sand at her Long Island estate when suddenly a huge wave rose up, broke over the beach and dragged the tot out to sea.

"Oh my God!" she shrieked. "Please, he's my only grandson. He's just three. I cannot lose him. It would destroy the family. Please, God can I have him back?"

No sooner had she finished her plea when another huge wave broke across the beach depositing the child safe and sound at her feet.

The grandmother looked up to the sky, held her arms wide and said, "He had a hat."

People say "I'm taking it one day at a time." You know what? So is everybody. That's how time works.

-Hannibal Buress

I was playing chess with my friend and he said, 'Let's make this interesting'. So we stopped playing chess.

-Matt Kirshen

Jerry was known to one and all of his friends as a bit of a crazy driver. He had gotten away with it for years until one day he was nailed for running a red light by one of those traffic cams.

A few days later, he opened the letter from the police department. It had a picture of him running the light and a fine of $100. Jerry mailed the return envelope back with a picture of two fifty-dollar bills.

A couple of days later he got another return envelope from the police with a picture of a pair of handcuffs.

Three old maids of a quite advanced age were living together in a creaky old house. One night, the 96 year-old went up and started drawing a bath. As she was getting in, she had a "senior moment" and suddenly couldn't remember whether she was getting out or getting in. She called downstairs to report her dilemma and the 94 year-old replied that she'd be right up to check.

About halfway up, the second old maid suddenly realized that she couldn't remember whether she was going up or going down so she called downstairs to ask.

The third old maid, who was 92, looked up from her knitting and thought, "I hope I never get as mentally foggy as those two," and rapped on the table to knock on wood.

"Hold on," she yelled. "I'll be right there- just as soon as I answer the door."

Rabbi Goldstein was sitting in his office when the Internal Revenue Inspector arrived for his appointment.

"I just have one question Rabbi," the agent said. "Murray Greenbaum claimed on his tax return that he donated $100,000 to your synagogue. I wanted to confirm that he did donate."

The rabbi thought for a moment and answered "Yes, yes he will."

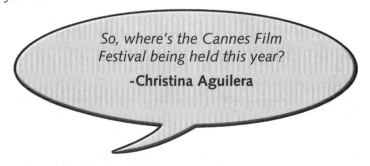

So, where's the Cannes Film Festival being held this year?

-Christina Aguilera

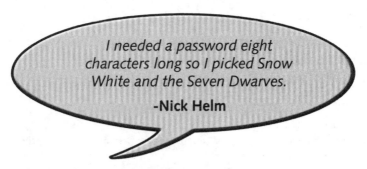

I needed a password eight characters long so I picked Snow White and the Seven Dwarves.

-Nick Helm

Jokepardy

Steve Allen did the bit as "The Question Man." Johnny Carson put on a turban and gave us "Carnac The Magnificent" for 30 years. Merv Griffin used the gimmick to create the classic game show "Jeopardy." And so with a respectful nod to the pioneers of this premise, we proudly present Joke-pardy. We give you the answer and you try to guess the question.

The answer is: Polynesia. And the question?
What do you call memory loss in parrots?

•

The answer is: Sis-Boom-Bah. And the question?
What's the sound of an exploding sheep?

•

The answer is: Good til the last drop. And the question?
What's a lousy slogan for a parachute company?

•

The answer is: Dewey Decimal System. And the question?
What do you get if you leave your Decimal System out all night?

The answer is: Gatorade. And the question?
What does an alligator get on welfare?

•

The answer is: Flypaper. And the question?
What's the best thing to use if you want to gift-wrap a zipper?

•

The answer is: Cyclone. And the question?
What can you grow from a single cell taken from a guy named "Cy"?

•

The answer is: Super Bowl. And the question?
What is it you'd find in Superman's bathroom?

•

The answer is: Chicken Teriyaki. And the question?
Name the only kamikaze pilot to survive the war.

•

The answer is: Pandemonium. And the question?
What do they call a retirement hi-rise for pandas in Florida?

To the people who've got iPhones: you just bought one, you didn't invent it!

-Marcus Brigstocke

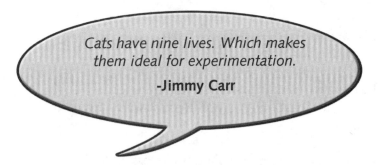

Cats have nine lives. Which makes them ideal for experimentation.

-Jimmy Carr

At the Rainbow Room, high up at 30 Rock, a woman noticed a very handsome young man sitting at the bar. She decided to break the ice by asking him what he was drinking.

"Magic beer," was his reply.

"I've never heard of magic beer," the woman purred.

"Here, I'll show you," the young man answered. With that he took a big gulp from the mug and then went out to the terrace and jumped off. The woman was totally shocked but a few seconds later he reappeared, hovering in mid air. He then topped the demonstration off with a quick fly around the skyscraper, landing safely back on the terrace.

"That's amazing!" the woman gasped.

"Would you like to try it?" asked the young man.

"Oh, I'd love to," was her enthusiastic response.

"Give her one of what I'm having," he said to the bartender, and she was handed a mug of cold beer.

She gulped it all down, then went out to the terrace and jumped, plummeting straight to her death.

The bartender shook his head and said to the young man, "You know, when you're drunk, you can be a real jerk Superman."

Harry had a bad hangover but he resolved to go to work anyway. As he was driving, half in a daze, his cell phone rang. It was his wife.

"Harry, I'm watching the local news. Be careful. They're saying that there's a nut out on the I-5 driving in the wrong direction."

Harry focused his eyes on the road ahead and replied, "One? It looks like there's hundreds."

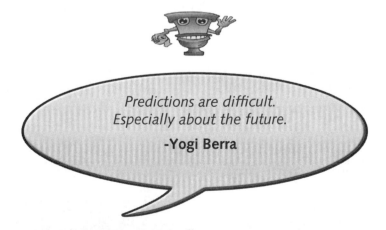

Predictions are difficult.
Especially about the future.

-Yogi Berra

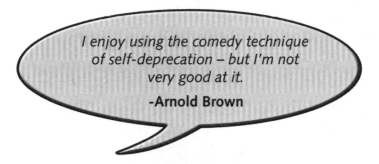

I enjoy using the comedy technique of self-deprecation – but I'm not very good at it.

-Arnold Brown

A group of teenage boys were hanging out at a video arcade when they noticed a young boy come in. "Hey look- it's Wilbur, the dumbest kid in town," Deke said with derision as he nudged his buddy in the ribs. "Dumber than dirt- here look."

With that he called Wilbur over to the group and motioned his friends to watch closely. "Hey Wilbur, look at this," Deke said as he held out his hands. One had a dollar and one had two quarters.

"Now, you take which one you want," Deke offered. Wilbur thought for a moment and then took the two quarters. Deke and his pals had a good laugh as Wilbur left the arcade.

Andy, the friendly arcade manager who happened to be watching the whole thing, followed Wilbur out the door. When he caught up he asked, "Wilbur, you're a smart enough boy. Why'd you take the two quarters?"

"Easy," said Wilbur. "Deke does that all the time. The day I take the dollar, the game's over."

Maxy Segal, serving 10 years in the pen, got a letter from his wife: "Dear Maxy, I wanted to grow some lettuce but since you're the one with the green thumb, I wondered when would be the best time to plant it in the garden."

Knowing that the guards read all the prisoner's mail, he replied: "My Dear Wife, whatever you do, don't dig up the garden. I buried the loot from the heist there!"

About a week later, Maxy received another letter from his better half: "Dear Maxy, I don't know what happened. A few days ago, fifty men with shovels showed up and dug up the entire garden."

Maxy sent his reply immediately: "My Dear Wife, it is now time to plant."

Two fish are swimming along a river in Idaho when all of a sudden, one bangs his head on a concrete wall.

"Dam!" he said.

If you're being chased by a police dog, try not to go through a tunnel, then on to a little seesaw, then jump through a hoop of fire. They're trained for that.

-Milton Jones

> *It is impossible to travel faster than the speed of light, and certainly not desirable, as one's hat keeps blowing off.*
>
> **-Woody Allen**

A woman was getting out of the shower and, as her husband was getting ready for his, the doorbell rang. The woman wrapped a towel around herself, went downstairs and answered the door. It was Larry, the next door neighbor.

Larry looked at her in amazement and said, "Oh, wow- I never realized that you were so beautiful! I'll give you $1,000 dollars if you drop that towel for just a few seconds."

The woman thought for a moment. Since they were having some money troubles, and her husband never need find out about it, she decided to go ahead with it. She dropped her towel and a bug-eyed Larry looked her up and down. He asked her to turn around and gave her another good looking over. He thanked her and gave her the $1,000.

The woman put her towel back on and went back upstairs. Her husband, fresh out of the shower, asked. "Who was at the door?"

"It was our neighbor Larry," she answered.

"Good," answered her husband. "Did he say anything about the grand that he owes me?"

An old guy crashed his cart into a younger man's cart at one of those huge bulk-buy warehouses. "Oh, I'm sorry," said the old man. "I was distracted. You see I've been trying to find my wife for the past half-hour."

"I know how you feel, " said the younger man. "I've been looking for mine for forty-five minutes and I'm getting a bit concerned."

"Well maybe we can help each other out," the old man said. "What's your wife look like?"

"She's 23, fantastic figure, green eyes, red hair and the prettiest face you've ever seen." the young man replied. "What's your wife look like?"

"Never mind that," the old guy replied. "Let's just look for yours."

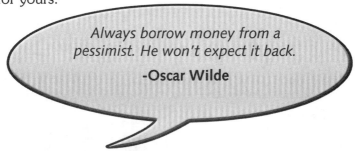

Always borrow money from a pessimist. He won't expect it back.

-Oscar Wilde

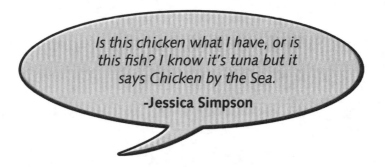

Is this chicken what I have, or is this fish? I know it's tuna but it says Chicken by the Sea.

-Jessica Simpson

Off the Wall

• *H lp! S m b d st l ll th v w ls fr m ths grfft !*

• *Velcro is a rip-off.*

• *WARNING: Dates On Calendar Are Closer Than They Appear*

• *This statement is false.*

• *There is no I in team- but there is in Independence.*

• *It's a small world -- unless you gotta walk home.*

• *Keep the dream alive: Hit the snooze button.*

• *I am the only one who can prevent forest fires.*

• *All things are possible- except skiing through a revolving door.*

- *Do unto others, then run.*

- *Why go to college? There's Google.*

- *You're only young once- but you can be immature forever.*

- *STOP REPEAT OFFENDERS!- Don't re-elect them.*

- *Why didn't Noah swat those two mosquitoes?*

Clete and Bo were sitting on the front porch admiring their collection of cars on blocks when a huge truck hauling turf rumbled by.

"Boy, that's one thing I'm going to do when I win the lottery," mused Bo.

"What's that?" asked Clete.

"Send my lawn out to get mowed."

> *Knowledge is knowing a tomato is a fruit; Wisdom is not putting it in a fruit salad.*
>
> **-Brian Gerald O'Driscoll**

*When people say "clean as a whistle",
they forget that a whistle is full of spit.*

-George Carlin

The first day on the new job, a budding lumberjack only managed to cut down three trees. While the boss wasn't too concerned, as time went on, no progress was made.

Finally, the boss called the lumberjack into his office for an interview to find out what the trouble was. "I don't understand it boss, I work as hard as I can- I don't even take breaks or lunch."

"Well son," his boss said understandingly, "maybe it's your equipment- could be your chain saw."

"No I checked that- it's sharp enough."

Checking to see if the saw ran properly, the boss pulled the cord and it cranked right up. Startled, the employee jumped a foot off his seat, looked around and shouted, "What's that noise?"

Did you hear about the invisible man and invisible woman's kids?
They're not much to look at.

In the hot, burning desert of Iraq, Private First Class McPherson was on his third tour of duty when he was observed to be acting oddly. All day long he would wander around picking up scraps of paper, declare, "That's not it" and frown as he tossed it away.

This went on for weeks until his commander ordered him to go for psychological evaluation. The psychiatrist noted his strange behavior and since he wouldn't answer any questions, he just observed him for a while. The disturbed soldier kept wandering around the shrink's office, picking up papers and discarding them, all the while muttering aloud, "That's not it."

After seeing enough of this behavior, the psychiatrist shook his head sadly and wrote out McPherson's discharge papers.

Just as the doctor signed them, McPherson ambled over to the desk, picked up the form and said, "That's it!"

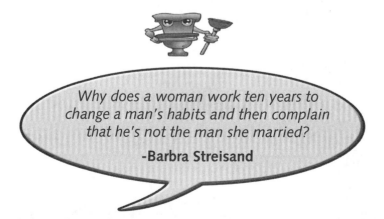

Why does a woman work ten years to change a man's habits and then complain that he's not the man she married?

-Barbra Streisand

> *I discovered I scream the same way whether I'm about to be devoured by a great white shark or if a piece of seaweed touches my foot.*
>
> **-Axl Rose**

A turtle was crossing a path in New York's Central Park when he was ambushed by a gang of snails. He was beaten up and robbed. After it was all over, a mounted policeman happened along and asked the turtle what had gone on.

"I don't know what to say, Officer," the turtle replied. "It all happened so fast."

"Doctor! Doctor!" the panicked patient gasped as he ran through the door. "You gotta help me- I'm shrinking!"

"Calm down," replied the M.D. "You'll just have to be a little patient."

Q: What do you get when you cross a Los Angeles freeway with a bicycle?
A: Killed.

Caller: Hello. I need an appointment with the doctor.
Receptionist: Okay. We have one open in...six weeks.

Caller: Six WEEKS? Are you nuts? I could be dead by then.

Receptionist: No problem. Then your wife can call and cancel.

Two women are having conversation over a cup of coffee and begin talking about their psychotherapists. One says, "My shrink drives me crazy. She answers every question with a question. Sometimes I think I'm just throwing good money after bad."

The other woman says, "I should be so lucky. I've been paying mine $300 a session for three years and he hadn't said one single word until yesterday."

"Really? What did he say?"

"No hablo Ingles."

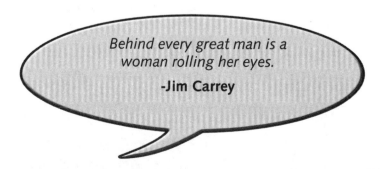

Behind every great man is a woman rolling her eyes.

-Jim Carrey

It's strange, isn't it? You stand in the middle of a library and go "aaaaagghhhh" and everyone just stares at you. But you do the same thing on an airplane, and everyone joins in.

-Tommy Cooper

Hasty Headlines

Culled from newspapers and web sites, they all have one thing in common: The editor should have taken time for another look.

Woman Missing Since She Got Lost

•

Drunks Get Nine Months in Violin Case

•

Kicking Baby Considered To Be Healthy

•

New Study of Obesity Looks for Larger Test Group

•

Statistics Show Teen Pregnancy Drops Off Significantly After Age 25

•

Woman Gets Shot On Lottery Show

Scientists Plan Mission To Probe Uranus

•

Teacher Strikes Idle Kids

•

One Armed Man Applauds
The Kindness Of Strangers

•

Hospitals Are Sued by 7 Foot Doctors

•

Two Convicts Evade Noose, Jury Hung

•

County To Pay $250,000
To Advertise Lack Of Funds

•

Crack Found On Governor's Daughter

•

Queen Mary Having Bottom Scraped

Smoking kills. If you're killed, you've lost a very important part of your life.

-Brooke Shields

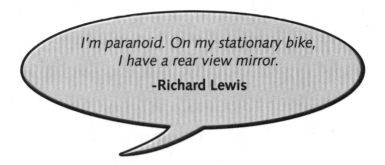

*I'm paranoid. On my stationary bike,
I have a rear view mirror.*

-Richard Lewis

An old guy saw some hoodlums attempting to make off with some tools from his backyard shed. He called the cops and said, "There are some thugs stealing stuff from my shed."

The police dispatcher replied, "All patrols are busy right now. Lock your doors and we'll be by when an officer is available."

The geezer waited a few minutes, then called again and said, "I called a little while ago about a couple of thieves in my shed, but don't worry. I've got a handle on it. I shot 'em both and my two pit bulls have got a really good grip on them."

Moments later, five police vehicles, a couple of fire trucks, a SWAT team and paramedics arrived and apprehended the burglars.

Afterward, one of the cops said to the old codger, "I thought you said you shot them."

The geezer answered, "And I thought you said no one was available."

A couple of young military recruits found three hand grenades on the road and decided to take them back to the base. "What if one of them explodes?" asks one of the recruits.

"No problem," says his army buddy. "We'll say we only found two."

First Goldfish: Do you believe in God?

Second Goldfish: Absolutely! Who do you think changes our water every day?

At the chapel, the groom stood beside his bride and his golf bag. A bit puzzled, his bride whispered, "What are your golf clubs doing here?"

The groom answered matter-of-factly, "This isn't going to take all day is it?"

Duct tape is like the force. It has a light side, a dark side, and it holds the universe together.

-Oprah Winfrey

Some people say that I must be a terrible person, but it's not true. I have the heart of a young boy in a jar on my desk.

-Stephen King

A quaint Irish pub had a little terrier as its mascot. The dog would drink beer from his bowl and clean up any scraps that hit the floor. One day the dog died suddenly. The owner decided to memorialize the pooch by cutting off his tail and leaving it on the pub's cash register.

Meanwhile, when the dog arrived at the Pearly Gates, St. Peter wouldn't let him enter because heaven is a place of perfection and the terrier's tail was missing.

So the dog went back down to the pub in the middle of the night to retrieve his tail, only to be told by the owner that it would not be possible. The dog asked why not and the owner replied, "It's illegal to retail spirits after hours."

Bill Gates appeared at the Pearly Gates where St. Peter said, "Allow me to escort you to your heavenly home." With that, Gates was brought to a little bungalow in the woods.

Right next door was a huge estate, complete with an Olympic size swimming pool, tennis court and a golf course. "My gosh. Who lives there?" Gates asked St. Peter.

"The captain of the Titanic," answered St. Peter.

"How come he gets a better eternal home than me?" asked Gates.

St. Peter replied, "Because the Titanic only crashed once."

Riley is in solitary confinement. The jailer walks by his cell, sees him hanging by his feet and yells, "What do you think you're doing?"

"I'm trying to commit suicide," says Riley.

"The rope is supposed to be around your neck."

"I know," says Riley, "but I couldn't breathe."

Doing nothing is very hard to do.
You never know when you're finished.

-Leslie Nielsen

> *My husband and I are either going to buy a dog or have a child. We can't decide whether to ruin our carpet or ruin our lives.*
>
> **-Rita Rudner**

A husband is on his way out to the store when the wife says, "Please pick up a carton of milk and if they have eggs, get me a dozen."

The husband returns home with 12 cartons of milk.

"Why on earth would you get me 12 cartons of milk?" asks the wife.

"They had eggs."

The owner of a small deli is complaining to the tax auditor, "Why don't you IRS guys leave me alone? I'm open every day, I work all kinds of hours, the whole family pitches in, and I only make $75,000 a year."

"It's not about your income, sir," says the tax man. "It's about your deductions. Five trips to the Caribbean?"

"We deliver."

A road crew foreman phoned the construction chief one morning. "Listen, Boss," the foreman moaned. "I don't know what we're going to do. The crew's all here but we got no shovels!"

"I'll send down some shovels immediately," the Boss responded. "In the meantime, have the men lean on each other."

Three little boys were walking to school when they saw a fire engine roar by with a Dalmatian sitting right up front. The first boy said, "They use Dalmatians to keep the crowds back."

The second boy said, "No, they just bring them along for good luck."

"Neither of you know what you're talkin' about," the third boy said, stopping the debate in its tracks. "They use them to find the fire hydrants!"

Those are my principles, and if you don't like them... well, I have others.

-Groucho Marx

The problem with the designated driver program, it's not a desirable job. But if you ever get sucked into doing it, have fun with it. At the end of the night, drop them off at the wrong house.

-Jeff Foxworthy

Sam and Jessie were meteorite hunters and heard about a big fall up in the Sierra Nevada Mountains. They grabbed their gear and a couple of plane tickets and flew to the town nearest the fall. Renting an all-terrain SUV, they drove to the debris field and started looking.

When they came home from the day's hunting, they stayed at a little motel that was gouging meteorite hunters $300 a night. They spent four days looking for meteorites but only found three tiny ones. Jessie was complaining about the poor results and said, "You know Sam, the way I figure it, these three tiny fragments cost us about $900 each."

"Well then," Sam replied. "You should be real happy we didn't find any more of them."

Four fonts walk into a bar. The bartender says, "Sorry, we don't allow any of your types in here."

Pranks for the Privy

As Joseph Gayetty, the inventor of toilet paper would say,"Let the good times roll" with these relatively harmless practical jokes for the john.

Give your toilet some pop by taping plastic bubble wrap on the underside of the lid and then gently put down the seat to await your victim.

•••

Unwind the toilet paper roll a few times, put a fake bug inside, and roll it back up again.

•••

For another paper caper, unwind about three sheets and glue the next piece to the rest of the roll. Wind it back up and press tightly to make sure the rolls sticks. Two sheets should be left dangling when the victim makes a futile attempt to unravel the roll.

•••

Buy a rubber worm. Get some fishing line, tie one end of it around the worm's head and tape the other end to the underside of the toilet seat for a lid-lifting laugher.

*Beauty fades . . .
dumb is forever.*

-Judge Judy

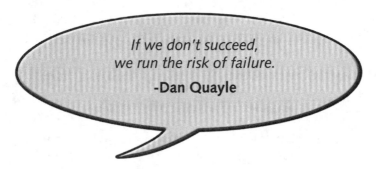

If we don't succeed,
we run the risk of failure.

-Dan Quayle

A guy goes into a seafood store with a salmon under his arm. He asks the owner, "Do you make fish cakes here?"

"Sure," says the fishmonger.

"Good. It's his birthday."

Carmella was one of the stars of the popular reality show *The Jersey Score*, but she was still cheap and bought herself a ticket in coach. Boarding the plane however, she went right up front and took a seat in first class.

After the plane was in flight, the flight attendant noticed that she was in the wrong seat and asked her to return to coach. "Listen," she told the flight attendant, "I'm blonde, I'm beautiful and I'm going to Hollywood."

The flight attendant went on with her duties but came back a few minutes later and whispered in Carmella's ear, "Please, you really must go back to coach."

Carmella repeated "I'm blonde, I'm, beautiful and I'm going to Hollywood." Then she reclined the seat to show that she meant to stay put.

The flight attendant tried several more times but was always met with, "I'm blonde, I'm beautiful and I'm going to Hollywood."

Finally, in total frustration, the flight attendant went forward to the cockpit and notified the captain. The captain emerged from the cockpit and went to Carmella's seat. Obnoxiously, she again repeated, "I'm blonde, I'm beautiful and I'm going to Hollywood."

The pilot leaned over and whispered in her ear. Almost immediately, Carmella got up from her seat and returned to coach.

"That's amazing!" the flight attendant gushed. "What did you say to her?"

"I simply told her," the captain grinned, "that this part of the plane wouldn't be going to Hollywood."

> Forget about the half-glass, half-full argument. More important is this: the bartender cheated you!
>
> **-Wayne Wright**

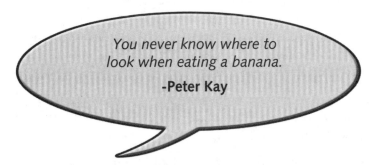

You never know where to look when eating a banana.

-Peter Kay

Two goldfish are in a tank. One says to the other, "You steer. I'll man the gun."

Once upon a time an evil witch placed a spell over a prince, whereby he could speak only one word a year. He was permitted, though, to save up words. If he didn't speak a word in a given year, for example, he would be allowed two words the next year.

One day the prince encountered an absolutely stunning princess and fell head over heels for her. He decided not to speak for two years so that he could look at her and say, "My sweetheart." At the end of the two years, however, he wanted to tell her that he also loved her, so he decided to wait three more years making for a total of five years of silence. Then, after five years, he knew he wanted to ask her to marry him, so he needed to wait four more years to speak- nine years in all. Finally, at the end of that period, the prince would be able to speak his piece.

With great anticipation, he led the princess into the royal garden where he knelt before her. He spoke those nine precious words that he'd waited nine long years to be able to deliver. "My sweetheart, I love you. Will you marry me?"

She replied, "Pardon?"

Two southern anglers decided to try their luck at something new and go ice fishing. Arriving in Minnesota, they stopped at the local bait and tackle shop and bought two ice picks before they went on to the frozen lake. They were back within the hour and bought a dozen more ice picks.

When they returned a third time and ordered every ice pick that was in stock, the curious proprietor asked, "So how are you boys doing?"

"Not very well," one answered. "We ain't even got the boat in the water yet!"

> *I told my psychiatrist that everyone hates me. He said I was being ridiculous – everyone hasn't met me yet.*
>
> **-Rodney Dangerfield**

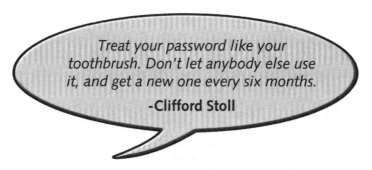

Treat your password like your toothbrush. Don't let anybody else use it, and get a new one every six months.

-Clifford Stoll

Oliver arrived home and told his wife, "I have a friend coming over for dinner."

"What?" his wife protested. "My hair is in curlers, the house is a mess, the kids are particularly noisy and wild and I was only going to serve something out of a box. Why on earth would you invite him over?"

Oliver answered, "Because he's thinking of getting married."

An elderly woman on her deathbed tells her grandson, "I want to leave my farm to you, dear. It includes the barn, the tractor, the harvest and livestock- oh, and $19,320,461.50 in cash."

The grandson is completely taken aback and says, "Awesome, Granny- thanks! And to think... I had absolutely no clue you even had a farm. Where is it?"

With her precious last breath, the grandmother whispered, "Facebook."

Four frat brothers were partying at night. As the evening wore on they realized they'd be ill-suited and ill-prepared to take their chemistry finals the next morning.

They hatched a scheme and showed up at the dean of students' office the next day, long after the exam class was over. One of the fraternity brothers, covered in grease, "explained" that they were late because their car blew a tire and the lugs were stuck. Try as they did, it took hours before they managed to change the tire.

The dean allowed for this and arranged for a makeup test in three days. This gave the boys plenty of time to cram for the exam.

On the morning of the make-up test, they were prompt and confident. The professor spaced them well apart from one other in the classroom so as to avoid any temptation to share information. He then handed out the exams in the envelope. When the students opened it, they found only two questions:

1.   Your name (two points)
2.   Which tire blew? (98 points)

The shortest distance between two points is under construction.

-Noelie Alito

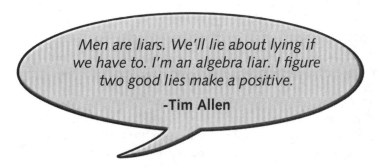

Men are liars. We'll lie about lying if we have to. I'm an algebra liar. I figure two good lies make a positive.

-Tim Allen

The hard-bitten detective was surveying the scene of his latest case. The victim was found in a bathtub filled with milk and he had a banana down his throat. A rookie cop assisting him was visibly shaken. "What kind of person could do a thing like this?" he moaned.

"What we are seeing here," the detective answered grimly, "is obviously the work of a cereal killer."

A woman says to the fitness instructor, "Can you teach me do to the splits?"

The instructor says, "Depends- How flexible are you?"

The woman says, "I can't make Thursdays."

A couple of birds are sitting on a perch. One says to the other, "Do you smell fish?"

Mr. Jeffers was giving a lesson on the body's blood flow to his eighth grade students. "Now I think you'll all agree," he began, "that if I stood on my head, all the blood would rush to it and my face would turn red."

His students all nodded in agreement.

"But how is it," he continued, "that if I stand upright, as I normally do, all the blood doesn't rush to my feet?"

From the back of the room, there came a voice, "Because your feet ain't empty!"

The captain of the royal vessel went down below the deck to address the slaves chained to the oars. "I have some good news and some bad news," he announced. "The good news is that the queen will be joining us today for an excursion on the waters. The bad news is that she wants to go water skiing."

> It's absolutely stupid that we live without an ozone layer. We have men, we've got rockets, we've got Saran Wrap – FIX IT!
>
> **-Lewis Black**

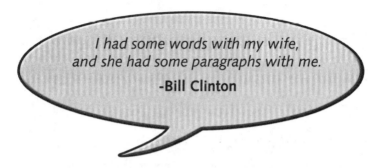

*I had some words with my wife,
and she had some paragraphs with me.*

-Bill Clinton

A Few Good Light Bulb Jokes

The wealthy light bulb manufacturer donated his products, free of charge, for use on all the theater marquees in New York. Seems he always wanted to see his lights up in names...

•••

How many drummers does it take to change a light bulb?

One- Two, and a-one, two, three, four...

•

How many stockbrokers does it take to change a light bulb?

Two- one to take the bulb out and drop it, and the other to try and sell it before it crashes.

•

How many car salesmen does it take to change a light bulb?

I have to work this out on my calculator but I think you will be pleasantly surprised.

How many archaeologists does it take to change a light bulb?

Three. One to change it and two to argue about how old the old one is.

•

One. How many psychics does it take to change a light bulb?

At a cocktail party, a doctor was standing with his wife when a beautiful girl with an outrageous figure shimmied by in the lowest cut, tightest gown the wife had ever seen. As she passed, the bombshell waved, said, "Well, hello there Doc," and went on her way.

Feeling his wife's eyes burning into him, the doctor cleared his throat and explained, "Don't worry dear, just a young lady I see professionally."

"That's what I thought," his wife answered with her eyes narrowing, "Your profession or hers?"

I dream of a better tomorrow- a tomorrow where chickens can cross the road and not be questioned about their motives.

-Scott Dellay

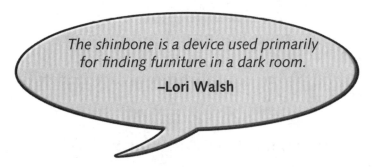

The shinbone is a device used primarily for finding furniture in a dark room.

–Lori Walsh

On a hot, dusty Midwestern day, a farm boy took his bat and ball out to a field and said to himself, "I'm the greatest batter in the world," and with that he tossed the ball in the air, took a swing and missed. Strike one!

Unperturbed, he repeated, "I'm the greatest batter in the world," tossed the ball, swung and missed. Strike two!

Once more, the farm boy dug in his feet, stated, "I'm the greatest batter in the world," tossed the ball in the air, swung and missed. Strike three!

"What do you know?" he said with surprise. "I'm the greatest pitcher in the world!"

Wife: Honey, I've got some good news and bad news about the car.

Hubbie: Gimme the good news first.

Wife: The air bag works.

Two kids who didn't make the cut for Abbott and Costello's "Who's on First?" baseball team were named Shut Up and Trouble. One day, Shut Up noticed that Trouble hadn't been around for a while and decided to go look for him. As he was walking down the street, a police car pulled alongside and the cop said, "Hey kid! What's your name?"

"Shut Up," the boy answered.

The cop, trying to hold his temper, said, "Answer the question boy. What's your name?"

"Shut Up," the boy repeated.

So the cop replied, "Say... are you looking for trouble?"

Shut Up perked up and excitedly asked, "Yeah! Have you seen him?"

Q: How does Moses make coffee?
A: Hebrews it.

I've never really wanted to go to Japan. Simply because I don't like eating fish. And I know that's very popular out there in Africa.

-Britney Spears

> *There's one thing that's really great about waking up early, and it's not jogging or greeting the day – it's just that that's when they make doughnuts.*
>
> **-Kathy Griffin**

A man runs into a psychiatrist's office. "Doctor! Doctor! You've got to help me. I think I'm a chicken."

"How long has this been going on?" the doctor asked.

"Since I was an egg."

Over at billionaire Warren Smorgasbord's mansion, sharks were kept in the swimming pool. It was a bit eccentric, but he could afford it, and with his kind of money he could do anything he liked.

One day, he realized that his unmarried daughter was approaching thirty and decided to throw her a huge poolside party. Invitations went out to every available bachelor in town.

On the big night, his estate was filled with young men. Beautiful ice sculptures festooned the poolside, and there was wonderful food and music. Suddenly, the host appeared and asked everyone for their attention.

"I want to announce a contest," he boomed over the mike. "I am prepared to offer a million dollars cash and my only daughter's hand in marriage to the young man who has the courage to swim across this swimming pool filled with sharks."

He looked over the crowd but there seemed to be no takers. Just then, there was a loud splash and sure enough, there was a young man swimming across the huge pool for all he was worth. The sharks were just about on him by the time he reached the other side and pulled himself out.

"Marvelous my boy, marvelous," beamed Smorgasbord. "I never thought anyone would do it but you proved me wrong young man. To you, a million dollars cash and my daughter's hand in marriage."

"I don't want your money and I certainly don't want your daughter," the man gasped trying to catch his breath.

"Then what do you want?" Smorgasbord asked.

"I want the name of the #&**%$#@$! who pushed me in the pool!"

Everyone should have kids. They are the greatest joy in the world. But they are also terrorists. You'll realize this as soon as they are born, and they start using sleep deprivation to break you.

-Ray Romano

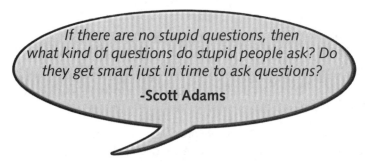

If there are no stupid questions, then what kind of questions do stupid people ask? Do they get smart just in time to ask questions?

-Scott Adams

Nuts to Soup...

One of the staples of the comedy menu in years gone by was the old 'Waiter, there's a fly in my soup...' gag, and some versions are truly enough to gag you...

"Waiter, there's a fly in my soup!"

"Please be quiet, Sir, everyone will want one!"

•

"Waiter, there's a fly in my soup!"

"How fortunate, Sir. There's usually only enough soup for them to wade."

•

"Waiter, there's a fly in my soup!"

"Don't worry, the tarantula will come up under him any moment now."

•

"Waiter, there's a fly in my soup!"

"I'm sorry, Sir, that's chicken noodle. You should have gotten the cockroach with that."

"Waiter, what's this fly doing in my soup?"

"Looks like the backstroke."

•

Frog: "Hey Waiter! There's no fly in my soup!"

•

"Waiter, there's a fly in my soup!"

"You're lucky that it's not a HALF a fly!"

•

"Waiter, there's a fly in my soup!"

"Oh, heavens no, Sir. He's not in your soup. He's been stuck to that bowl for weeks!"

•

And to a server who just spilled a bowl of steaming broth in an annoyed customer's lap, "Waiter, there's a soup in my fly!"

•

"Waiter, waiter! I need some coffee without cream."

"I'm sorry, sir, but we're out of cream. Would you like it without milk instead?"

A cannibal is a guy who goes into a restaurant and orders the waiter.

-Jack Benny

> *I have six locks on my door all in a row. When I go out, I lock every other one. I figure no matter how long somebody stands there picking the locks, they are always locking three.*
>
> **-Elayne Boosler**

A lawyer, meeting with his client in prison, says, "I've got some good news and bad news."

The client says, "Gimme the bad news first."

"Your DNA matches the blood found on the victim as well as the murder weapon."

"What could the good news possibly be?" asks the client.

"Your cholesterol is down to 120."

A retired couple lived at their beachfront house. All summer they watched a woman on the beach approach people, take something out of her bag and give it to them, then collect money and leave.

"Drug dealer!" the wife concluded. "I'm going to call the police."

"Hold on, Honey," her husband protested. "We don't know that."

As the summer wore on, the wife observed that the woman only approached people with boom boxes or portable video games.

"Get our boom-box out of the attic, Dear," the wife ordered. "Tomorrow we are going down to the beach and are going to get to the bottom of this once and for all."

The next day the couple set up on the beach with their boom box and waited for the woman to come by. Sure enough, she approached the husband and whispered something in his ear. He shook his head "no" and she went on her way.

When she got out of earshot, the wife anxiously asked her husband, "Well? Was it drugs?"

The husband shook his head and said "No, batteries."

"Batteries?" the wife repeated incredulously.

"Yes dear," the husband smiled. "She sells "C" cells by the seashore."

I've always wanted to go to Switzerland to see what the army does with those wee red knives.

-Billy Connolly

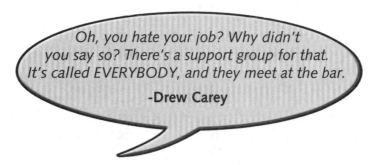

Oh, you hate your job? Why didn't you say so? There's a support group for that. It's called EVERYBODY, and they meet at the bar.

-Drew Carey

A blind guy went into a bar, climbed up on a stool and asked the bartender if he'd heard the latest blonde joke.

The bartender went over to him and said, "Mister, I want to be fair to you. Before you tell that joke, I have to warn you that I'm a blonde. The guy next to you is a blonde ex-pro football player. The waitress behind you used to be a stuntwoman and is well versed in karate and many other martial arts and she's a blonde. And finally, Tiny over in the corner is a six-foot-eight pile of muscle topped off with a thick crop of blonde hair. Now do you still want to tell that joke?"

"Heck no," the blind man replied. "Not if I'm going have to explain it four times!"

A fellow is driving down a heavily flooded road after a torrential rainstorm when, all of the sudden, he sees a guy's head sticking out of a huge puddle. He stops and asks the guy if he needs a ride. The guy answers, "Nah, that's ok. I'm on my bike."

Willy was getting ready for his first parachute jump. The last thing his instructor said to him was, "Remember Willy, once you're out, count to five and pull this cord for the primary chute. If that fails, pull this cord for the backup chute. Keep your legs loose when you land and while you roll up your chute, a truck will head out to get you."

With that, the instructor pushed Willy out of the plane. Willy counted to five and then pulled the cord for his main chute. It didn't deploy so he pulled the cord for his back-up chute. It didn't deploy either.

As Willy was plummeting towards the earth, he thought, "Great! The way my luck's been going today, the truck's probably not gonna show up either."

Teacher: If you stood facing north and your back was due south, what would be on your left hand?

Little Johnny: Fingers.

> *I don't kill flies but I like to mess with their minds. I hold them above globes. They freak out and yell, "Whoa, I'm way too high!"*
>
> **-Bruce Baum**

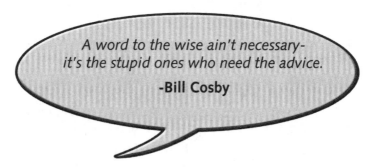

A word to the wise ain't necessary-
it's the stupid ones who need the advice.

-Bill Cosby

A bunch of ostriches decided to throw a surprise birthday party honoring one of their own down by the lake. At the appointed hour, the lookout ostrich looked down the lakeshore and saw the birthday bird approaching. "Here he comes!" the lookout ostrich whispered. "Quick everybody, get your heads in the sand!"

Two cars traveling in opposite directions collided one foggy night on a backcountry road. It wasn't a head-on but there was extensive damage to both vehicles. The drivers got out and introduced themselves. One was a doctor, the other one a lawyer.

"I've already called the police," said the lawyer. "They should be here in about fifteen minutes."

"Good," the doctor replied.

"Sure is cold out here," the lawyer observed.

"Sure is," the doctor replied.

Pulling out a flask of brandy, the lawyer offered the
doctor a drink to keep him warm.

"Thanks," said the doctor as he took a few big gulps.
He handed the flask back to the lawyer but the lawyer
just tossed it into his trunk.

"Aren't you going to have a nip?" asked the doctor.

"Maybe after the police get here," grinned the lawyer.

A one armed man walked into a second-hand store.
The owner said, "I don't think you're going to find what
you're looking for here."

A woman says to her physician, "Doctor you have to
help me- I think I'm addicted to Twitter."

"Sorry," the doctor replied. "I don't follow you."

*The chicken came first –
God would look silly sitting on an egg.*

-Roy Harry

Speed up airport security lines and body scans. Fly naked!

-Cesar DaGama

Bumper Snickers

• Cover me. I'm changing lanes.

• I Brake For No Apparent Reason.

• BAD COP! - NO DONUT!!

• If you can read this, I can slam
on my brakes and sue you!

• Forget world peace. Visualize using your turn signal.

• My Hockey Mom Can Beat Up Your Soccer Mom

• Honk if you love peace and quiet.

• Your kid may be an honor student
but you're still an IDIOT!

Levi had a rich uncle who was on the verge of death. He had, at most, weeks to live. Being his only living relative, Levi stood to inherit $100,000,000 and he wanted to find a woman to share it with.

One night he went out to a bar and spotted the most beautiful woman he had ever seen. Breathless at her beauty, Levi gasped, "You are a goddess and although I'm just an ordinary man, in a few weeks I'll inherit $100,000,000. Would you consider going home with me?"

Not blinking an eye, the woman took his arm and they went home together. Sure enough, three weeks later, she became his stepmother.

Reverend Bob was nothing if not resourceful. He went to his church one rainy Sunday morning and announced to his congregation, "I've got good news and bad news. The good news is that we have all the money we need to fix this leaky roof. The bad news is it's still out there in your pockets."

What I look forward to is continued immaturity followed by death.

-Dave Barry

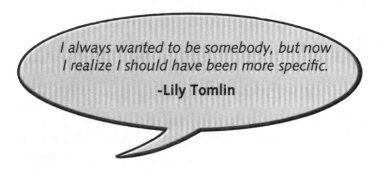

I always wanted to be somebody, but now I realize I should have been more specific.

-Lily Tomlin

"I'm getting married!" gushed the starry-eyed young yam.

"To whom?" asked Mother Yam.

"Brian Williams."

"Brian Williams of NBC-TV? You can't marry him!"

"Why not?" demanded her daughter.

"Because you are a yam and he's just a commen-tator."

Two mathematicians from the same city were invited to a conference and wound up sitting together on a plane. One seemed nervous and uncomfortable. "What's wrong?" asked his seatmate.

"Oh, it's all this terrorism business. It makes me nervous. Do you know what the odds are that there's a bomb on this plane?"

"Yes I do," replied the other mathematician. "I've actually calculated it out. "On any given flight the odds are a thousand to one against there being a bomb on board."

"A thousand to one?" the nervous mathematician replied. "Forgive me but those odds aren't that good."

"Yes, I know," said the other math whiz. "But the good news is that the odds jump to ten million to one against there being two bombs on the same plane."

"Well that makes perfect sense," replied the nervous mathematician, "But how is that supposed to make me feel any better?"

"Easy," his friend said, opening his carryon bag. "I always pack my own bomb!"

Q: If H20 is the formula for water what is the formula for ice?
A: H20 cubed

> *Marriage is nature's way of keeping us from fighting with strangers.*
>
> **-Alan King**

> *Thank you Facebook, I can now farm without going outside, cook without being in my kitchen, feed fish I don't have & waste an entire day without having a life.*
>
> **-Unknown**

On a long flight overseas, a lawyer was getting bored so he decided to shake things up a bit for his own amusement. The lovely passenger in the seat next to him had a thick southern drawl and the lawyer thought that her clothes made her look like a perfect bumpkin. Being always quick to judge by appearances, the attorney challenged her to a game of wits.

"Oh no," she protested. "I'm sure you'd win. I've never been any good at that sort of thing."

The lawyer pressed her. "C'mon- I'll give you ten to one odds. I will ask you a question and if you cannot answer it, you pay me $10. Then you ask me a question, if I can't answer it, I'll give you $100."

"Well, all right," the Southern lady answered. "But I'm just doing this to be polite."

The lawyer grinned and hit her with his question, "In miles, how far is it from the Sun to the next-nearest star?"

The woman sighed and handed the lawyer $10.

"Okay, it's your turn," the lawyer stated with confidence.

The woman thought for a moment and said, "What goes up a hill with two hats but comes down with only one?"

The lawyer was stunned. He had once been a champion on "Jeopardy" and was a member of MENSA but he was positively stumped. He spent the next two hours wracking his brain and searching the computer. Finally, in total defeat and frustration, he handed the woman a $100 bill, which she placed in her purse.

"Come on," the lawyer insisted. "I just paid a hundred dollars to know. What goes up a hill with two hats but comes down with only one? What's the answer?"

The Southern Belle smiled and handed him another $10.

Q: What do you get when you cross a turkey with a centipede?
A: Drumsticks for everyone.

My fake plants died because I did not pretend to water them.

–Mitch Hedberg

> *I found there was only one way to look thin: hang out with fat people.*
>
> **-Rodney Dangerfield**

Potty Ponderings

You might want to use your personal down time to ponder these great questions of the Universe...

• Is a vegetarian allowed to eat animal crackers?

• If you choke a Smurf, what color does it turn?

• What do you say when an atheist sneezes?

• How would you do the YMCA in Chinese?

• Why do you press harder on a remote control when you know the battery is dead?

• What happens if you get scared "half to death" twice?

• How come you never see the headline "Psychic Wins Lottery"?

• Why is a carrot more orange than an orange?

• If you were given an order to disobey all orders would you disobey that order?

• Ever stop to think, and forget to start again?

• When they arrest a mime, do they say, "You have the right to remain silent"?

• What happened to Preparations A through G?

• What exactly is the speed of dark?

• What was the best thing before sliced bread?

• If you melt dry ice can you take a bath without getting wet?

• Is there another word for "synonym"?

Mary had a little lamb. The doctor fainted.

> *Just because nobody complains doesn't mean all parachutes are perfect.*
>
> **-Benny Hill**

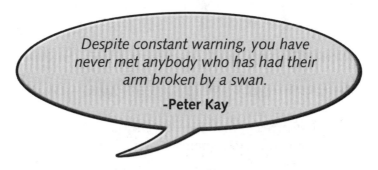

Despite constant warning, you have never met anybody who has had their arm broken by a swan.

-Peter Kay

A man was riding a bicycle built for two all alone when he was pulled over by the police. "What's the problem, Officer?" he asked.

"Perhaps you hadn't noticed but your wife fell off a half-mile back," the officer replied.

"Oh, thank God," the bicyclist said as he wiped his brow. "I was afraid that I had gone deaf!"

Fireman Jim was visiting an elementary school with his presentation on fire safety. To start off he held up a smoke detector and asked, "Does anyone here know what this is?"

One hand in the back of the room went up and Fireman Jim called on little Johnny. "Do you know what this does?"

"Yeah," Johnny answered. "It's how mommy knows dinner is done."

TV newswoman Diane Foyer called up the British ambassador and asked him what he'd like for Christmas.

"I can't accept any gifts," he said diplomatically.

Ms. Foyer persistently suggested that he could have anything he wanted, big or small. The ambassador finally relented and said, "Well, I suppose I could accept a small box of chocolates."

That night, the ambassador was watching the network news when he heard Lawyer say, "We asked a number of dignitaries what they'd like for Christmas. The French ambassador said he'd like world peace. The German ambassador wished prosperity for the poor. And the British ambassador would like a tiny box of candy."

One guy says to another, "I think I want a Labrador."

His pal warns, "That might not be such a good idea. Have you seen how many of their owners go blind?"

Two things are infinite: the universe and human stupidity; and I'm not sure about the universe.

-Albert Einstein

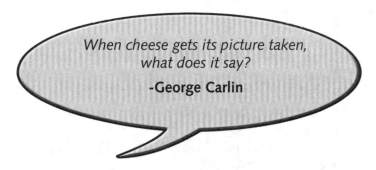

When cheese gets its picture taken, what does it say?

-George Carlin

A businessman was in the airport VIP lounge when he spotted Donald Trump standing at the bar. He went up to The Donald, introduced himself and said, "Mr. Trump, you've always been a hero of mine. It's great to meet you."

Trump smiled and shook his hand. The businessman then said, "I was wondering if you could do me a tiny favor?"

"Shoot," said Trump.

"Well I'm here to meet a client. I'm at that table over there and when she gets here it would be a great help if you just strolled by the table and said 'Hi Bob.'"

"Sure," said Trump.

A couple of minutes later, the client arrived and had barely taken her seat when Trump stopped at the table and said "Hi Bob."

The businessman shot an angry glance at him and replied, "Get lost Trump, I'm in a meeting!"

The night court judge was mass-dispensing justice when he got to the case of a young fellow who pleaded guilty to robbing a liquor store. "Have you ever been in trouble before?" asked the judge.

"Just once," replied the young man. "I once stole from my kid brother's bank."

"Well, that doesn't sound serious," said the judge.

"My brother thought it was," answered the defendant. "It cost him his job as president of Wells Fargo!"

The teacher was asking the class about what their parents do for a living. "What does your Daddy do?" Mrs. Jones asked Little Johnny.

Little Johnny replied, "My daddy's dead."

"Oh, I'm sorry," said Mrs. Jones. "But what did he do before he died?

"He sort of grabbed his chest and fell over."

I really don't think I need buns of steel. I'd be happy with buns of cinnamon.

-Ellen DeGeneres

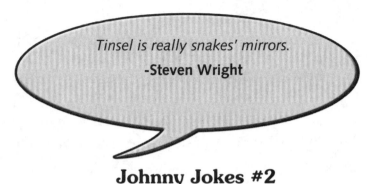

Tinsel is really snakes' mirrors.
-Steven Wright

Johnny Jokes #2

A husband and wife were having a real set-to and after it was over, the husband noticed how calm his wife was.

"Stella," the husband said, "How is it that no matter how much we fight, you stay calm, cool and collected?"

"Easy," his wife replied."Whenever we fight, I take out all my hostilities by cleaning the bathroom."

"Cleaning the bathroom?" her husband replied incredulously. "How does that help?"

His wife just smiled and said,"I use your toothbrush."

•••

Figuring she had a few minutes to run errands before the plumber arrived, a woman slipped out but as luck would have it, just a moment later the plumber showed up and knocked on the door.

"Who is it?" the lady's pet parrot piped up, the only phrase, by the way, that the bird had ever learned.

"It's the plumber!" came the cordial reply.

"Who is it?"

"It's the plumber!!" the man shouted.

"Who is it?"

"IT'S the @#%&! PLUMBER!" the tradesman screamed, jumping up and down in frustration on the porch. Suddenly, he had a massive heart attack and collapsed in front of the door.

Just then the woman returned home. Seeing the body on her porch, she exclaimed, "Heavens! Who is it?"

And the parrot chimed in with, "It's the plumber!"

•••

There was a rootin-tootin cowboy who sashayed to the outhouse in back of the saloon. He heard a noise coming from inside and looked down the hole. Sure as shootin', there was an old Indian looking back up. The cowboy offered him a hand and said, "Poor fellah. How long have you been stuck down in that awful hole?"

The Indian answered sadly, "Many moons."

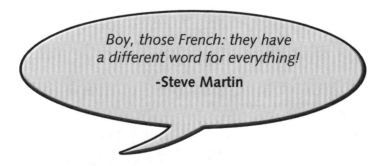

Boy, those French: they have a different word for everything!

-Steve Martin

> People say New Yorkers can't get along. Not true. I saw two New Yorkers, complete strangers, sharing a cab. One guy took the tires and the radio; the other guy took the engine.
>
> **-David Letterman**

Late at night, a doctor got an emergency phone call from one of his patients.

"Doc, listen, it's my wife. I think she's got appendicitis!"

"That's impossible!" replied the doctor somewhat annoyed at being disturbed for a false alarm.

"No, Doc, I'm tellin' ya, it seems like it's appendicitis," retorted the husband.

"Couldn't be," explained the doctor in a very condescending manner. "I took your wife's appendix out last year. Now, have you ever heard of anyone getting a second appendix?"

"Well, no, Doc," came the reply. "But have you ever heard of anyone getting a second wife?"

One penguin says to the other, "You look like you're wearing a tuxedo."

The other replies, "Who says I'm not?"

While doing research on a South Pacific Island, a scientist discovered a a rare bird in the jungle that, through years of contact with missionaries, had learned to speak ten different languages. He was amazed and shipped the prized bird home to his wife in a special cage as a surprise anniversary gift.

A month later he arrived home from his expedition. His wife welcomed him with the news that in celebration of his arrival, she had cooked the bird as the main course in his welcome home dinner.

"You cooked the bird I sent home from the South Pacific!?" the man shouted. "It spoke ten languages!"

"Ten languages?" replied his surprised wife. "He should have said something."

Q: Why is Facebook a good site for loners?
A: Because it's the only place where they can talk to a wall and not be considered a loser.

> Guys are lucky because they get to grow mustaches. I wish I could. It's like having a little pet for your face.
>
> **-Anita Wise**

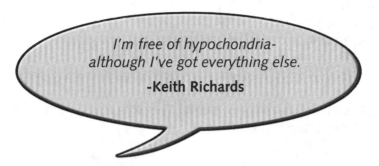

I'm free of hypochondria-
although I've got everything else.

-Keith Richards

Jack and Mimsy were celebrating at a night spot and the martinis had been flowing heavily all evening long. Suddenly, Jack slid off his chair and under the table.

"Pardon me Madam," the waiter said. "But your husband has just slipped under the table."

"That's not exactly the case." slurred Mimsy. "My date just slipped under the table. My husband just walked through the door."

Two buddies met at a bar and one asked the other how things were going.

"Not so hot- had an argument with the wife," was his answer.

"What happened?" asked his friend sympathetically.

"We had money troubles so she told me I couldn't buy beer by the case anymore."

"Then I caught her paying $50 a bottle for nail polish off a TV shopping channel."

"That's not right."

"Yeah and then, she went to a beauty parlor and had a $250 makeover."

"So what'd you do?"

"I confronted her and demanded to know why she was wasting all that money."

"What did she say?"

"She said that she had to. She needed all that stuff so that she could look prettier for me."

"What'd you say?"

"I said 'Are you crazy? That's what the beer was for in the first place.'"

Happiness is your dentist telling you it won't hurt and then having him catch his hand in the drill.

-Johnny Carson

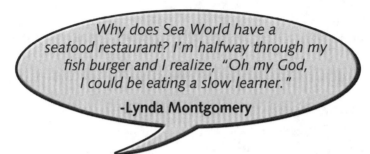

Why does Sea World have a seafood restaurant? I'm halfway through my fish burger and I realize, "Oh my God, I could be eating a slow learner."

-Lynda Montgomery

Thoughts of the Throne

"I come from the kind of family where my mother kept an extra roll of toilet paper on the tank in back of the toilet, and it had a little knit hat with a pom-pom on it. I didn't know if the purpose of this was so people wouldn't know that we had an extra roll of toilet paper or because my mother felt even toilet paper was embarrassed to be what it is." *-Jerry Seinfeld*

•

"My wife was immature. I'd be at home in my bath and she'd come in and sink my boats." *-Woody Allen*

•

"My plumbing is all screwed up. Because it turns out, I do not own a garbage disposal." *-Demetri Martin*

•

"Buckingham Palace has 78 bathrooms. Apparently, the Queen likes a lot of thrones." *-Sanford Mims*

•

"I grew up with six brothers. That's how I learned to dance – waiting for the bathroom." *-Bob Hope*

"Men who consistently leave the toilet seat up secretly want women to get up to go the bathroom in the middle of the night and fall in." *-Rita Rudner*

•

"Life is like a movie- since there aren't any commercial breaks, you have to get up and go to the bathroom in the middle of it." *-Garry Trudeau*

•

"I sometimes feel alone and insignificant, especially when people turn out the lights while I'm still in the bathroom."
-Steven Wright

A drunk staggers into a bar and yells, "Happy New Year!"

The bartender says, "Hey, buddy, it's not January first. It's Groundhog Day."

The drunk slurs, "Oh no... My wife is gonna kill me!"

If your name is on the building, you're rich; if your name is on your desk, you're middle-class; if your name is on your shirt, you're poor.

-Rich Hall

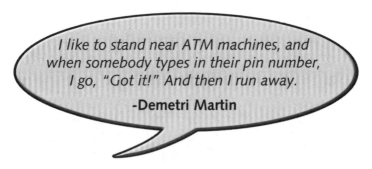

I like to stand near ATM machines, and when somebody types in their pin number, I go, "Got it!" And then I run away.

-Demetri Martin

The prune-faced old Dean of Women was addressing the freshman class at orientation.

"The female dormitory is out-of-bounds for all male students. For the first violation, men will be fined $50, the second violation will cost you $150, the third violation is $300."

"Let's stop beating around the bush Dean," came a voice from the back row. "How much is it for a season pass?"

Gladys burst thought the front door of her home shouting, "Pack your bags I won the lottery!"

"That's great!" exclaimed her husband. "Should I pack them for warm weather or cold?"

"I don't care," said Gladys gleefully. "Just get the heck out!"

Three racehorses were bragging about their accomplishments to one another.

"Out of 22 races, I won 12," said the first.

"Oh yeah?" challenged the second." Out of 30 races, I won 24."

"That's nothing," replied the third. "I ran 42 races and won 39."

A greyhound who had been standing nearby decided to join in. "Not bad fellas, but out of 100 races, I won 99. What do you think of that?"

The horses look at one another in amazement and then the first horse said, "Wow! A talking dog!"

A penguin waddled into a bar and said, "Was my dad here today?"

The bartender replied, "I dunno. What does he look like?"

Sometimes I wonder whether the world is being run by smart people who are putting us on, or by imbeciles who really mean it.

-Mark Twain

Airplane travel is nature's way of making you look like your passport photo.

-Al Gore

Two executives, a man and a woman, were mistakenly assigned to the same sleeper on a train on their way to a convention. After much embarrassment, they decided to accept the situation and get some sleep. In the middle of the night, the man leaned down from his upper birth and tapped the woman.

"I'm awfully sorry to disturb you but I'm very cold. Could you hand me that blanket over there?"

"I have a better idea," the woman replied. "How about, just for tonight, we pretend we're married?"

"Great!" said the man, brightening.

"OK," replied the woman. "Now get your own blanket!"

Chester: A man knocked on my door today and asked for a small donation for the local swimming pool.

Lester: What did you give him?

Chester: A glass of water.

Horrible Hector, the infamous pirate, terrorized the Spanish Main for many years with his ever-faithful mongrel at his side. That dog was his only soft spot. Hector was tremendously proud of the fact that he had taught the dog to bark once for "Si" and twice for "No".

Eventually Horrible Hector's fortunes changed and one day the Spaniard found himself surrounded by the British fleet. He and his ship were sent to Davy Jones' Locker but the pooch was saved.

The British Commodore adopted the mongrel and taught him the same trick only in English. And so, that lowly pirate's pooch went down in history as the world's first "Si" and "Aye" dog.

A guys walks into a bar and orders a Manhattan. When the bartender serves him the drink, the guy points to the big hunk of parsley in the middle of it and says, "What the heck is that?"

"Central Park."

Freshman congressmen spend the first week wondering how they ever got there and the rest of their term wondering how everyone else ever got there.

-Unknown

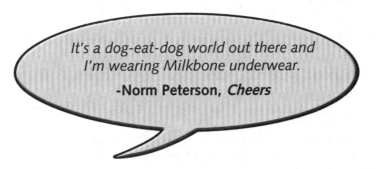

It's a dog-eat-dog world out there and I'm wearing Milkbone underwear.

-Norm Peterson, *Cheers*

A tourist walked down a filthy back alley of Manhattan and into a dingy antique shop. While perusing the goods, a bronze rat caught his eye. It wasn't very attractive but somehow, it called to him and so he asked the old man behind the counter how much it was.

"The rat sir, is twenty dollars but the story behind it will cost you a thousand," the old man replied.

"Keep your story, I just want the rat," the tourist said as he slipped the money across the counter.

"Very well then," the old man replied as he wrapped up the rat.

The tourist was hardly out of the alley when he noticed two rats following him. A block later, there were twenty. The man quickened his pace but the rodents kept up with him, more rats joining in with every trash can, alley and abandoned car they passed.

The tourist was walking as fast as he could with the hundreds of rats staying hot on his heels. Eventually he broke into a full run with thousands of rats streaming out of every tenement and sewer.

Gasping for breath and with tens of thousands of rats in hot pursuit, the tourist dashed down a pier, shinnied up a lamppost and tossed the bronze rat statue as far as he could into the harbor.

In a scene reminiscent of the Pied Piper, the rats climbed over each other to follow the bronze rat into the water. In a few minutes it was all over- all the rats had drowned and the tourist slipped back down the lamppost and made his way back to the dingy antique store.

"Ah- you're back," observed the old man behind the counter. "I'll bet you came back for the story," he said.

"I'm really not interested in the story," the tourist replied. "I just want to know if you have any bronze lawyers."

Q: What's the difference between a lawyer and a liar?
A: The pronunciation

I saw a sign at a gas station. It said "help wanted." There was another sign below it that said 'self service.' So I hired myself. Then I made myself the boss. I gave myself a raise. I paid myself. Then I quit."
-Steven Wright

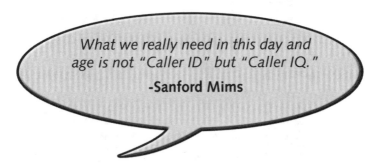

What we really need in this day and age is not "Caller ID" but "Caller IQ."

-Sanford Mims

Tim had just begun his new job delivering pizza and as luck would have it, his first delivery was to old Miss Scone, a woman famous all over town for being a skinflint.

When she answered the door, he presented her with the pizza. She said, "Now I suppose you want a tip. Tell me, how much do you usually get?"

"Well ma'am," answered Tim, "everybody told me that I'd be lucky to get a dime out of you."

"They did did they?" Miss Scone answered, a bit insulted.

"Well, you tell them all that you got five dollars young man," she said as she put the money into Tim's hand.

"Thank you Miss Scone! I'll put it right in my college fund."

"College?" She inquired."What are you studying?"

Tucking the money into his pocket, Tim answered with a smile, "Applied Psychology."

Chuck Norris Jokes

Chuck Norris doesn't need an introduction!

• Chuck Norris can slam a revolving door.

• Chuck Norris sneezes with his eyes open.

• Chuck Norris won *American Idol* using only sign language.

• Chuck Norris can speak in Braille.

• Chuck Norris can chew water and describe the taste of it.

• Chuck Norris knows Victoria's Secret.

• Chuck Norris can watch new episodes of *Seinfeld*.

• Chuck Norris counted to infinity - twice.

• Chuck Norris is the reason why Waldo is hiding.

I asked God for a bike, but I know God doesn't work that way. So I stole a bike and asked for forgiveness.

-Emo Philips

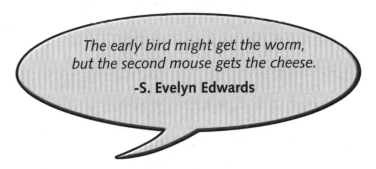

The early bird might get the worm, but the second mouse gets the cheese.

-S. Evelyn Edwards

Patient: Doc, you gotta help me. My wife thinks she's an elevator.

Psychiatrist: Bring her in to see me.

Patient: I can't. She doesn't stop on this floor!

Three old maids arrived at the Pearly Gates just in time for St. Peter's orientation lecture.

"I'd like to welcome you all to Heaven and point out that we have one rule and one rule only: Never step on a duck. Never. Violation of this rule will be severely dealt with."

The three old maids entered Heaven confident that they could avoid stepping on any ducks. Almost immediately, however, one managed to do it. St. Peter appeared with an incredibly ugly hobgoblin and chained it to the old maid.

"This is your punishment for stepping on a duck-chained to this hideous beast for all eternity."

As they were walking to their new quarters, the second old maid heard a sickening sound and realized that she too had stepped on a duck. Again St. Peter appeared and chained her to a hobgoblin.

This left a great impression on the third old maid and she resolved to walk with great care and never step on a duck. She was still obeying St. Peter's rule, many years later, when St. Peter showed up at her door with an incredibly sexy young man. He was Brad Pitt, George Clooney and Ryan Reynolds all rolled into one. St. Peter proceeded to chain them together and then left without saying a word.

When she got over her shock, the old maid gazed upon the young man and gushed, "Oh, I can't imagine what I've ever done to deserve this!"

The gorgeous young hunk replied,"I don't know about you lady, but I stepped on a duck."

A committee is a group that keeps minutes and loses hours.

-Milton Berle

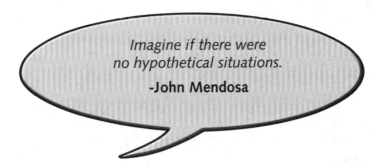

*Imagine if there were
no hypothetical situations.*

-John Mendosa

Down at the stationhouse, a rookie cop hauled a little guy up in front of the sergeant. The man had a desk strapped to his back, was carrying a water cooler under his right arm, a laptop under his left arm and was wearing a fax machine for a hat.

"What's the charge, Murphy?" growled the crusty old desk sergeant.

"Impersonating an office, sir."

Watching the evening news, Harry was irked by an item that Stefi Vavoom, his favorite actress, had married a pro basketball player who was well-known for his sleazy and arrogant personality.

"I'll never understand why the biggest jerks always get the most beautiful women!" Harry huffed.

His wife blushed and said, "Why thank you, Harry."

"Doc, I can't figure out what's wrong with me. I woke up today and called my wife Minnie. I put on some white gloves and on my way out the door started whistling, 'Hi ho, hi ho, it's off to work I go.' Then at the office I called my boss Grumpy and my secretary Cinderella."

"Not to worry- it's nothing major," says the doctor. "You're having Disney spells."

Patient: Doc, everybody takes advantage of me!

Psychiatrist: That's quite normal.

Patient: Really? That's great! How much do I owe you?

Psychiatrist: How much have you got?

Q: What do you call a monkey in a minefield?
A: A Baboom!

A day without sunshine is like, you know, night.

-Steve Martin

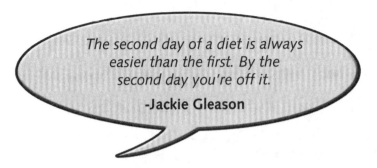

The second day of a diet is always easier than the first. By the second day you're off it.

-Jackie Gleason

The lawyers were called into the judge's chambers for a conference.

"I want you to know," the judge began, "that I have received bribes from both of you. Twenty-five thousand coming from McGrath and thirty thousand from Schwarz."

The lawyers squirmed in their seats fearful of what was next.

"I have decided," said the judge while pulling out his checkbook, "that the only fair thing to do is return five thousand to Schwarz and then go ahead and decide the case on its merits."

A husband and wife are sitting on their porch watching the sunset, sipping a glass of wine.

After a while the wife says, "I love you so much. I don't know how I could ever live without you."

The husband says, "Is that you talking ? Or the wine?"

She says, "It's me talking. *To* the wine."

A guy dashes into a psychiatrist's office, throws himself to the couch and says, "Doc, ya gotta help me, I think I'm a biscuit. What do you think?"

The shrink stokes his chin thoughtfully and asks, "Are you square?"

"Yes."

"Do you have lots of little holes?"

"Yes!, Yes!"

"And are you covered all over with a light sprinkling of salt?"

"Yes!, Yes!, Yes!"

"Then you're not a biscuit---you're crackers!"

Patient: Doctor, I just ate an orange ball, a red ball and a blue ball. I feel horrible!

Doctor: No wonder. You're not eating enough greens!

I guess I just prefer to see the dark side of things. The glass is always half empty. And cracked. And I just cut my lip on it. And chipped a tooth.

-Janeane Garofalo

I was thinking about how people seem to read the Bible a whole lot more as they get older. Then it dawned on me... they're cramming for their final exam."

-George Carlin

Mad Ribs

Do-it-yourself jokes- just fill in the blanks with your favorite target.

Q: Why did the _____ buy a box of Cheerios?
A: She thought they were bagel seeds.

Q: Why do _____ have "TGIF" printed on their insoles?
A: It helps them remember Toes Go In First.

Q: Why can't _____s dial "911"?
A: They can never find the "11" key.

Q: How do you break a _____'s finger?
A: Punch him in the nose.

Q: Why couldn't the _____ learn to water ski?
A: Because he/she couldn't find a lake with a slope.

Q: Why did the _____ woman baste the turkey for five days?

A: The instruction said "one hour per pound" and she weighed 130.

Q: What did the _____ say when the pizza man asked him if he wanted his pizza cut into six or eight slices?

A: "Six- I could never eat eight!"

Did you hear about the _____ who tried to blow up a car? He burned his lips on the exhaust pipe.

Then there was the _____ who was fired as proof-reader at the M&M factory. He kept throwing out all the Ws.

Did you hear the one about the _____ who returned the scarf he got as a Christmas present? It was too tight.

A vegetarian is a person who won't eat anything that can have children.

-David Brenner

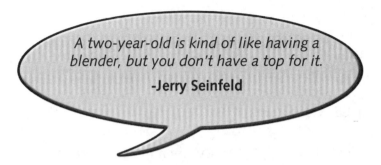

A two-year-old is kind of like having a blender, but you don't have a top for it.

-Jerry Seinfeld

A loving and devoted couple were looking forward to the big Halloween costume ball for some months and even went so far as to rent matching gorilla costumes. When the time came to leave, however, Louise was stricken with one of her killer migraines, but insisted that her husband go on ahead without her.

After an hour nap, Louise was feeling better. She put on her costume and went to the party, excited about how surprised her husband would be.

Spotting the other gorilla, Louise walked up and motioned him to the terrace. The two gorillas danced together and then Louise gave a few fetching gorilla grunts, took his hand and led him out onto the deserted beach. Soon, with the moonlight working its magic, they were locked in a passionate embrace, gorilla suits and all—and engaging in monkey business of the highest order.

After their tryst, the two gorillas walked hand in hand back to the party to mingle but Louise, exhausted from her workout, took the opportunity to slip away and returned home.

Later, when her husband came home from the party, he found her propped up in bed reading. Deciding to play it coy, Louise purred, "How was the party, Dear?"

"Okay, I guess," came his rather noncommittal replay.

OKAY, YOU GUESS?" She was highly insulted. "What do you mean by that?"

"Well, I couldn't get into it without you, Honey, so I spent the evening playing poker in the back room."

Then he brightened and added, "But wait till you hear what happened to the guy I loaned the costume to!"

A woman calls in sick to work. Her boss asks, "What's wrong?"

She says, "I have occupational glaucoma."

"What's that?" he asks.

"I just can't see coming into work today."

> Food, love, career, and mothers-
> the four major guilt groups.
>
> **-Cathy Guisewite**

Coffee isn't my cup of tea.

-Samuel Goldwyn

The king is moose hunting in the woods with one of his henchmen. Suddenly, they spot another fellow a distance away. The king raises his rifle and aims it at him. The fellow yells out, "I am not a moose!!!"

The king fires at the man and kills him. "Your highness!" his startled henchman exclaims. "He said he wasn't a moose!"

The king says, "Oh- I thought he said, 'I am a moose.'"

A floozy and her floo-zer were walking down the street when she spotted a lovely overcoat in a store window.

"Oooooo, I'd love that coat!" purred the young lady to her companion.

Without batting an eye, he picked up a brick, smashed the display window, retrieved the coat and draped it over her shoulders as they walked on. A short time later, they passed a jewelry store.

"Oooooo, I'd love that diamond ring," she cooed, admiring a rock not too terribly much smaller than Gibraltar. Without saying a word, her Galahad picked up a brick, smashed the window, plucked the precious stone from the debris and placed it on her dainty finger.

They walked on a short distance and as they turned a corner, she caught sight of a brand new Mercedes sports car gleaming in a showroom window.

Putting on her sexiest voice, the glamour girl whispered, "Oooooo, I'd love that beautiful Mercedes."

Her boyfriend stopped, turned around and snapped, "Hey whaddya think I'm made of- bricks?"

The math teacher noticed that little Johnny was daydreaming in class. She startled him by saying, "Johnny! What are 4 and 7 and 36 and 52?"

Little Johnny gathered his wits quickly and replied, "FOX, ABC, ESPN and the Cartoon Network."

A bank is a place that will lend you money if you can prove that you don't need it.

-Bob Hope

> *Not all chemicals are bad. Without chemicals such as hydrogen and oxygen, for example, there would be no way to make water, a vital ingredient in beer.*
>
> **-Dave Barry**

Barney is meeting with his priest. "Father," he says, "My psychiatrist says I have a split personality, but I still want to get married."

The priest says, "I don't see anything wrong with that, Barney. Who is it that you want to marry?"

"The Murphy twins."

Two auto dealers discussing the economy were trying to one-up each other about how bad business was.

"I tell you, George, business is terrible. I only sold one car yesterday."

"Oh, yeah?" retorted George. "Well, I also only sold one car yesterday and today itнs even worse!'"

"Geez, how could it be worse than that?" asked Charlie.

"Today," answered George, "the customer returned it!"

Q and A

Q: Why do fire departments have Dalmatians?
A: To help them find hydrants

Q: Why does Snoop Dog always carry an umbrella?
A: Fo' Drizzle

Q: What did one fly say to the other fly?
A: Hey, fly, your dude is open.

Q: What happens if you don't pay your exorcist?
A: You get repossessed.

Q: What's red and not there?
A: No tomatoes.

Q: What do you get if you divide the circumference of a pumpkin by its diameter?
A: Pumpkin pi.

I went to watch Pavarotti once. He doesn't like it when you join in.

-Mick Miller

> *Did you ever notice when you blow
> in a dog's face he gets mad at you?
> But when you take him in a car he sticks
> his head out the window.*
>
> **-Steve Bluestein**

Q: Why did the dinosaur cross the road?
A: Chickens hadn't been invented yet.

Q: Why did the lollipop cross the road?
A: It was stuck to the chicken.

Q: What's the difference between one yard and two yards?
A: A fence.

Q: Why do elephants paint their toenails red?
A: So they can hide in cherry trees.

Q: What do you get when you cross an elephant with a skin doctor?
A: A pachydermatologist

Q: What does DNA stand for?
A: National Dyslexic Association

A beautiful young woman arrived home to find her apartment had been broken into and ransacked. Almost hysterical at this violation of her home, she called the police and a K-9 unit nearby responded within the minute.

The officer knocked at her door with the police dog on its lead and showed his ID. At this, the woman became even more upset, breaking down and sobbing uncontrollably. When she finally calmed down, the officer asked her what was wrong.

The woman sniffed back her tears and wailed, "Being burglarized is bad enough. Now they send me a blind policeman!"

Larry: My wife kept hinting that she wanted to go somewhere expensive for our anniversary.

Harry: So where'd you take her?

Larry: To a gas station.

The trouble with political jokes is that very often they get elected.

-Will Rogers

I tried to walk into Target but I missed.
-Mitch Hedberg

A guy who was tired of being called "monkey-puss" inherited $10,000 and decided that he'd invest it in improving his unsightly appearance.

He went to a plastic surgeon, plunked down the cash and said, "Give me whatever you think I need the most."

A few hours later, he woke up in the recovery room and ran to the mirror. His face was just as bad as ever. He could tell that he didn't have a tummy tuck or hair transplant either, so he barged back into the surgeon's office and demanded to know what he got for the money.

"Well, my good fellow, you asked me to give you whatever you needed most and I did," replied the doctor.

"Yeah?" came the belligerent reply. "Then where is it?!?"

"Look behind you," said the surgeon. "I added a tail!"

Did you hear about conjunctivitis.com?
It's a site for sore eyes.

Tenant: I want to make a complaint about my upstairs neighbors. Last night they were shouting and banging on the floor until all hours of the night!

Landlord: I'm sorry. Did they wake you up?

Tenant: No. Fortunately, I was up late practicing on my tuba.

One day at the Customs counter, an agent suspiciously eyed a bottle hidden in the luggage of a tourist returning from Europe.

"And what's this, Ma'am?" he asked.

"Oh, it's just a bottle of holy water from Lourdes," said the sweet little old lady.

The inspector uncapped the bottle, took one whiff and said, "Whiskey!"

"Whiskey?" cried the woman. "Glory be to the highest! Another miracle!"

If you live to be one hundred, you've got it made. Very few people die past that age.

-George Burns

> *A good rule of thumb is if you've made it to thirty-five and your job still requires you to wear a name tag, you've probably made a serious vocational error.*
>
> **-Dennis Miller**

A truant officer noticed little Johnny playing in a front yard during school hours.

"Tell me, Son, is your mother at home?"

"She sure is," was Johnny's polite reply.

The truant officer rapped on the door but there was no answer. He rapped once again, waited and knocked once more. Still no answer. He pressed the door bell and waited, all the while watching the boy playing in the yard.

Finally, the truant officer walked completely around the house, tapping on all the windows and calling for the boy's mother but there was still no answer.

After 15 minutes, the exasperated truant officer said to little Johnny, "Son, are you absolutely sure that your mother is at home?"

"Yep, I sure am, Mister."

"Then why doesn't she answer the door?"

"'Cause this isn't our house!'"

The Bathroom Horoscope

See where you fit into the Bathroom Zodiac and find out if your life is going to be a royal flush or if you're destined to just circle the drain.

Aries (March 21 - April 19) The Toilet Seat
Born under the sign of the Toilet Seat you are doomed to have bad luck. If life were a two-story outhouse, you'd always be the person on the first floor.

Taurus (April 20 - May 20) The Faucet
Those born under the sign of the Faucet have two unfortunate character traits. Either you're "tight" all the time or just a big drip. This leads members of the opposite sex to find that once you are turned on, you're all wet.

Gemini (May 21 - June 20) Toilet Paper
You are born under the sign of Toilet Paper and like toilet paper, your life will be long and useful. Also like toilet paper, as long as you're on a roll, things are fine but once you're not, an unkind fate awaits you.

A new survey says that 47% of people believe that astrology has some scientific proof. I don't believe in astrology because I'm an Aries and we are really skeptical.

-Conan O'Brien

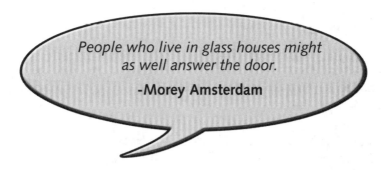

People who live in glass houses might as well answer the door.

-Morey Amsterdam

Cancer (June 21 - July 22) The Flush Handle
You are known to one and all to be easy going. Perhaps too easy going. In fact, you really should look into adult diapers. As a Flush Handle, you have the type of personality that can set things in a whirl but whenever anything goes down, you are above it all.

Leo (July 23 - August 22) The Mirror
People born under this sign are often vain and tend to go into the business world. Expect to be presented the key to the Executive Wash Room very soon. It will come with a bucket of cleaning supplies and a mop.

Virgo (August 23 -September 22) The Bath Tub
You will fight a serious weight problem all your life. You'll be the only one on your block who has stretch marks on their bathtub. Eventually you'll need to butter the sides. Also, as you are a Bath Tubian, most of your life you will find yourself in hot water.

Libra (September 23 - October 22) The Towel Rack
Born under the sign of The Towel Rack, you are fated to spend your life serving in a support capacity to various hangers-on. Because of this, you often get a screw loose or come unglued and go totally off the wall.

Scorpio (October 23 - November 21) The Medicine Cabinet
You have had a strained relationship with the bathroom all your life. Your only hope is to eat more fiber. The Medicine Cabinet is an appropriate sign as most people consider you to be a real pill.

Sagittarius (November 22 - December 21) The Throne
Those born under this sign tend to pinch pennies. You are the type to install a super low flow toilet just so you can get 3000 flushes.

Capricorn (December 22 - January 19) The Wash Cloth
Men born under this sign tend to be a Don Juan with the ladies. The women Don Juan to have anything to do with them. Female Wash Cloths on the other hand, tend to look like a million bucks- after taxes.

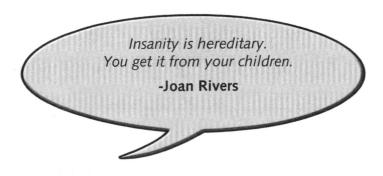

Insanity is hereditary.
You get it from your children.

-Joan Rivers

People seldom live up to their baby pictures.

-Rodney Dangerfield

Aquarius (January 20 - February 18) The Bowl
Born under this sign you have always concentrated on your career and have worked yourself up into a pretty big gun at the office. The downside is that they are planning to fire you soon.

Pisces (February 19 - March 20) The Blow Dryer
Those born under the sign of the Blow Dryer tend not to the sharpest knives in the drawer. They tend to be hired by mind readers wishing to go on vacation. They're the only ones in the Bathroom Zodiac who can trip over cordless phones and who think that an innuendo is an Italian suppository.